NOTEBOOK

RULED PAPER

THIS BOOK BELONGS TO:

Made in the USA
Thornton, CO
12/09/22 12:53:56

fc3b6654-f389-4499-bc21-e524b19c3d8eR01